ZONDERKIDZ

A Night of Great Joy

Copyright © 2016 by Mary Engelbreit Enterprises, Inc.

Requests for information should be addressed to:
Zonderkidz, 3900 *Sparks Dr. SE, Grand Rapids, Michigan* 49546

ISBN 978-0-310-74354-5

16 17 18 19 20 / LPC / 22 21 20 19 18 17 16 15 14 13 12 11 10 9 8 7 6 5 4 3 2

FOR

WITH
LOVE
AND
THANKS

SR. MARGARET MARY

But the angel said to them, "Do not be afraid.
I bring you good news of great joy. It is for all the
people. Today in the town of David a Savior has
been born to you. He is Christ the Lord."
—Luke 2:10–11 (NIrV)

A NIGHT OF GREAT JOY

MARY ENGELBREIT

ZONDER**kidz**

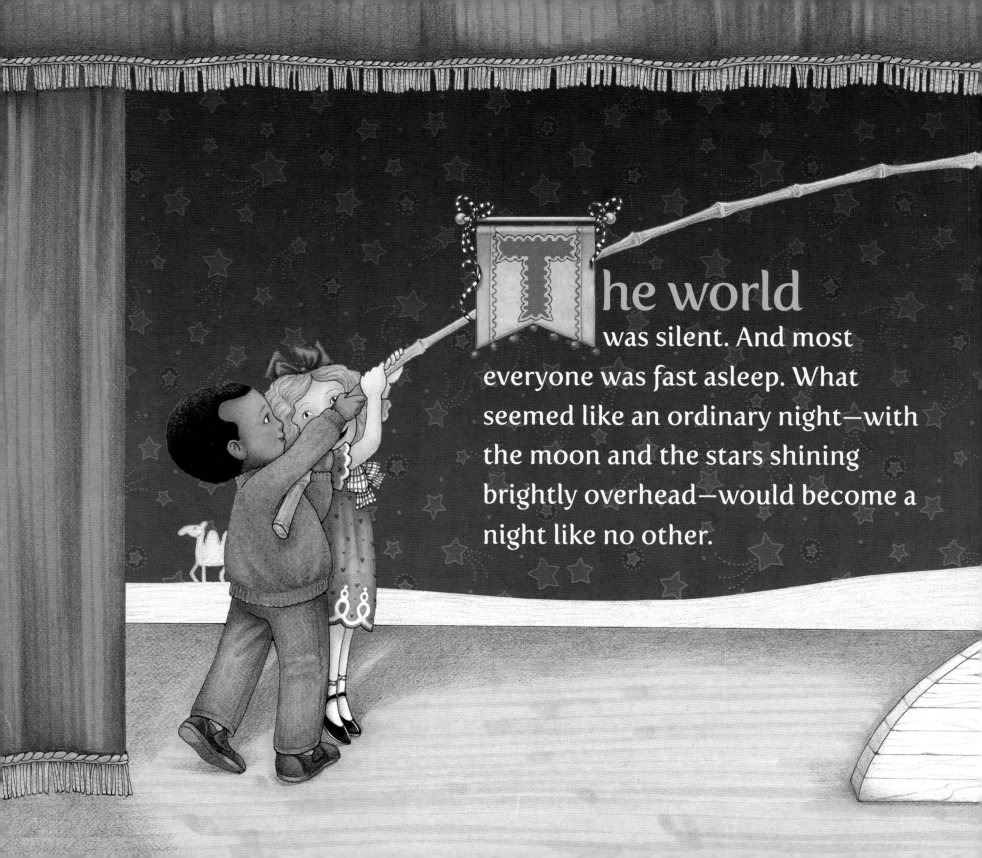

The world was silent. And most everyone was fast asleep. What seemed like an ordinary night—with the moon and the stars shining brightly overhead—would become a night like no other.

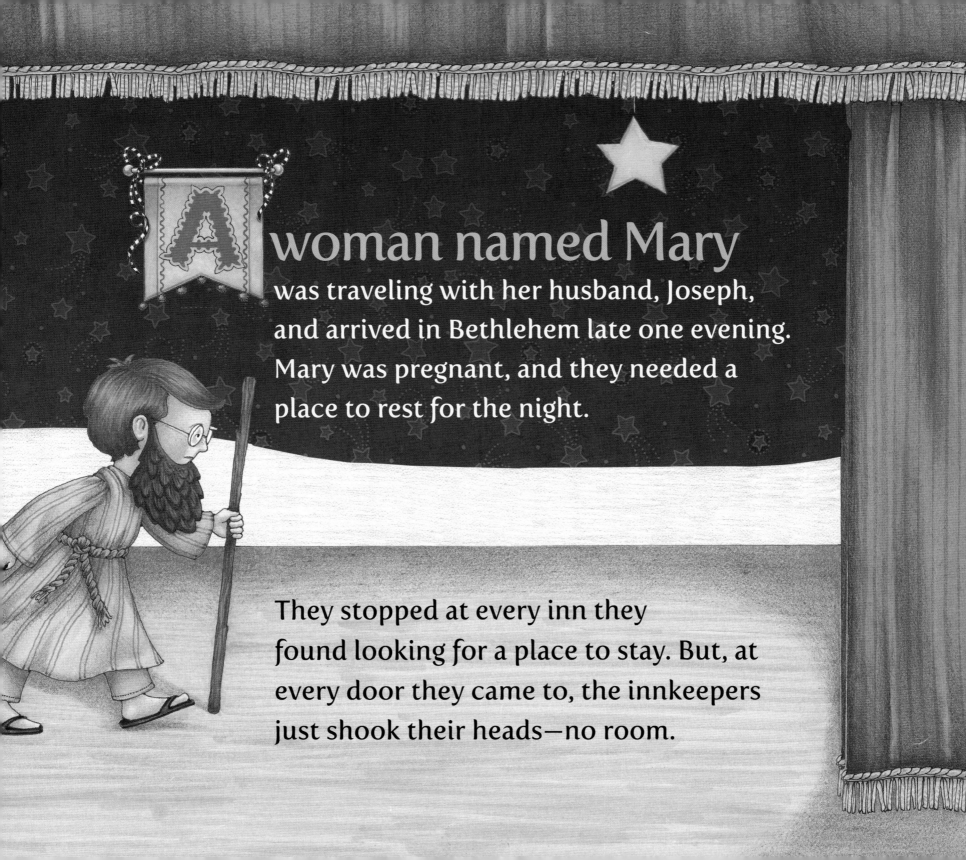

A woman named Mary was traveling with her husband, Joseph, and arrived in Bethlehem late one evening. Mary was pregnant, and they needed a place to rest for the night.

They stopped at every inn they found looking for a place to stay. But, at every door they came to, the innkeepers just shook their heads—no room.

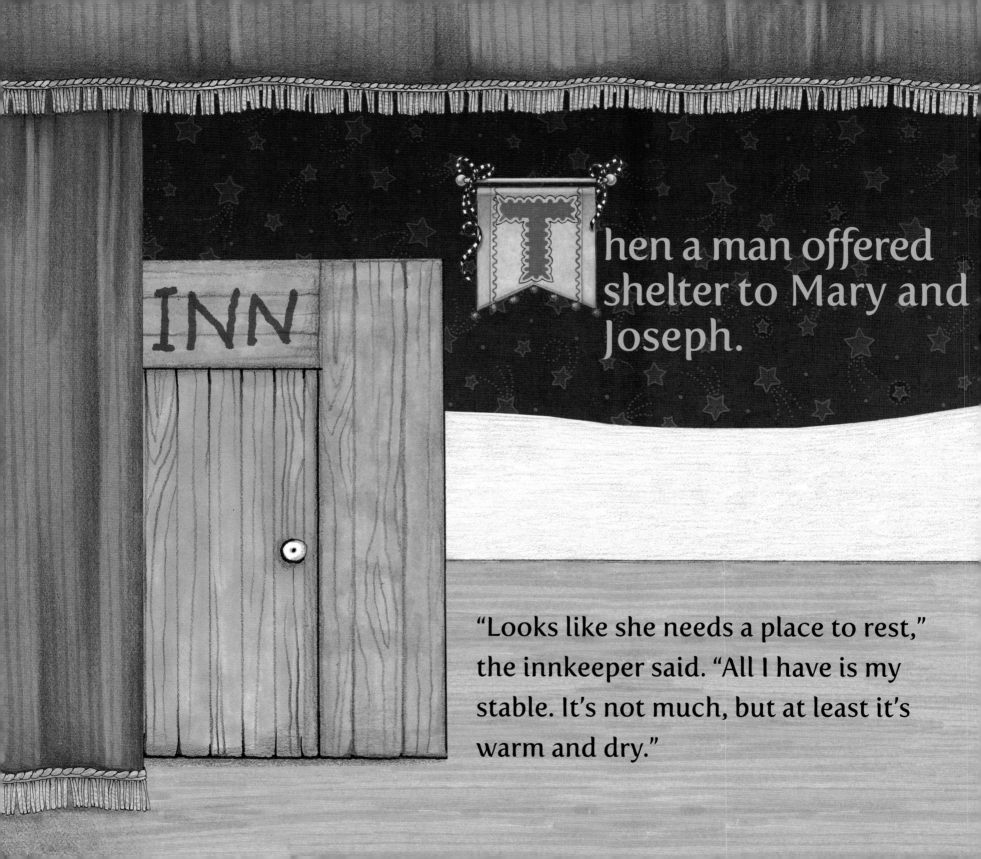

INN

Then a man offered shelter to Mary and Joseph.

"Looks like she needs a place to rest," the innkeeper said. "All I have is my stable. It's not much, but at least it's warm and dry."

Finally, they had a place to rest.

Although it was only a stable for oxen, cattle, and donkeys, it was just right. Joseph helped Mary down from the donkey. With great relief, she lay on a bed of straw.

That night, Mary gave birth to God's only son. His cries in the night echoed through the quiet streets of Bethlehem.

ello, Jesus," Mary whispered as she looked down at her precious baby boy.

Then she gently laid him upon the straw in a wooden manger. Mary and Joseph felt blessed that God had chosen them to care for this very special baby.

The animals

gathered close, in awe of God's great gift.

Not far away, there were shepherds caring for their sheep on a hillside.

Suddenly a bright light shone, and an angel appeared before them. "Don't be afraid," said the angel. "God has sent me to tell you the greatest news."

"This very night, a Savior
is born in the city of David!"

Then the night burst into brilliant light and beautiful sound as hundreds of angels filled the sky.

"Glory to God!" they sang. "Peace on earth
and goodwill to all mankind!"

Far off in the east, three wise men saw a brilliant star and knew it would lead them to the newborn king.

The wise men traveled to Bethlehem with precious gifts
of gold, frankincense, and myrrh. Gifts fit for a king!

All those gathered under that bright star were filled with joy, and knelt down to worship the child.

At last, the Savior of the world had come.

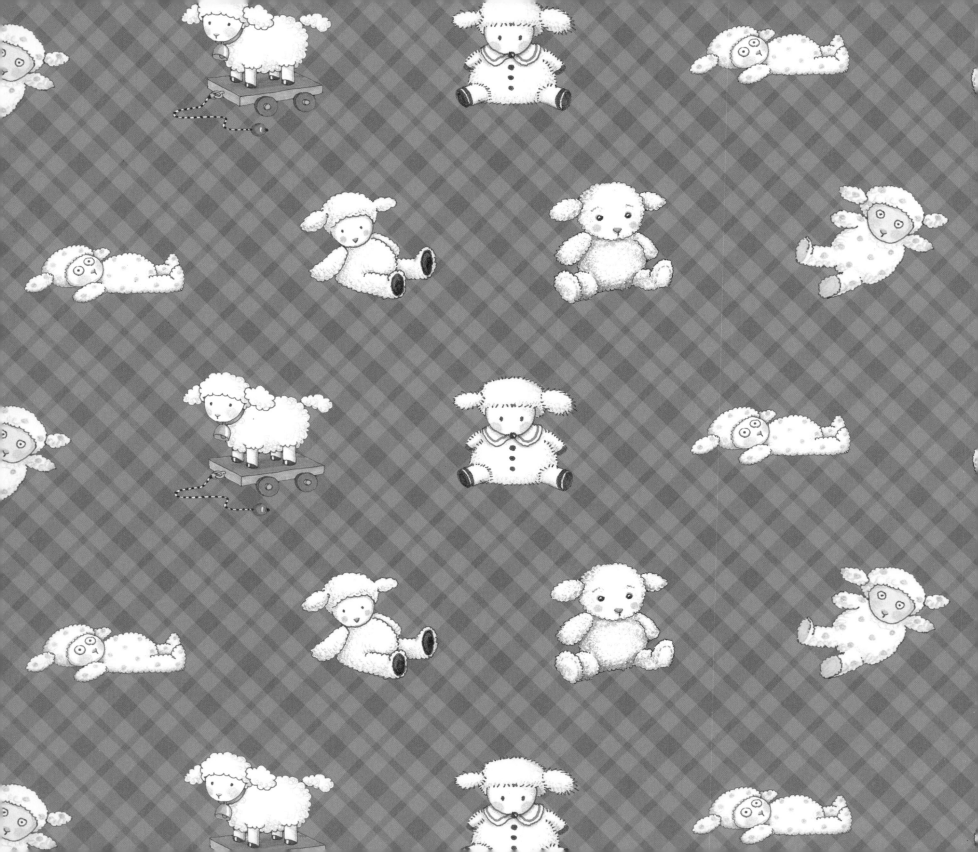